FIRST PARTNER'S
SUMMER BOOK CLUB

Nina

"When I die . . . I'm gonna know that I left something for [my people] to build on. That is my reward."

—NINA SIMONE,
Morehouse College, 1969

To my parents. —T.N.T.

For Nina. —C.R.

G. P. Putnam's Sons

An imprint of Penguin Random House LLC, New York

First published in the United States of America by G. P. Putnam's Sons, an imprint of
Penguin Random House LLC, 2021

Visit us online at penguinrandomhouse.com

Library of Congress Cataloging-in-Publication Data is available.

Manufactured in China

ISBN 9781524737283
10 9 8 7 6 5 4 3 2 1

Design by Eileen Savage. Text set in Fritz Book.
The art was created with acrylic paint, collage, and a bit of digital manipulation.

This is a work of nonfiction. Some names and identifying details have been changed.

words by **TRACI N. TODD**

pictures by **CHRISTIAN ROBINSON**

Nina

A Story of Nina Simone

putnam

G. P. Putnam's Sons

Eunice Kathleen Waymon came into this world on February 21, 1933, in the small town of Tryon, North Carolina.

She wasn't the first Waymon child, or the last, but she was the only one who sang before she could talk and found rhythm before she could walk. The only one with music on the inside.

There was music on the outside, too. Mama was forever singing church songs as she baked the biscuits and stirred the beans. And Daddy played the small upright piano.

Sometimes, when Mama was away, Daddy sat Eunice on his knee and put her fingers atop his as he played his favorite good-time jazz. Eunice learned so quickly, it wasn't long before Daddy was lounging on the porch, listening to Eunice play all on her own.

Then suddenly, Daddy would whistle—*Quick! Mama's coming!*—and Eunice would slip into Mama's favorite hymn without missing a note.

Mama was a minister and thought jazz was unholy music. She preached all day Sunday, and sometimes Wednesday, in proper churches and backwoods shacks. When Eunice was three, Mama brought her along to play the music of the Lord.

She played softly at first, letting Mama warm her flock. As Mama's power grew, Eunice matched her rhythm, rolling, rolling, until at last the congregation was on its feet, overcome by the message and the music.

When she wasn't preaching, Mama worked as Mrs. Miller's maid. She didn't love the job, but she had many mouths to feed and not a lot of choices. To pass the hours, she liked to tell Mrs. Miller how talented Eunice was.

When at last Mrs. Miller heard Eunice play, she knew the little girl had a gift. So she introduced Eunice to her friend, a piano teacher named Muriel Mazzanovich.

The next Saturday, Eunice walked three miles to Miss Mazzy's house. It was deep in the woods and a world away. There were lemon drops, sunlight in the ceiling, and a shiny grand piano.

Miss Mazzy taught Eunice to curl her fingers, straighten her back, and play *concertos* and *fugues. Classical music*, Miss Mazzy called it, written long ago for kings and queens. The music of Johann Sebastian Bach was Eunice's favorite. She liked the way it started softly, then tumbled to thunder, like Mama's preaching.

WHITE ONLY

After her lessons, Eunice walked to Mrs. Miller's house. While she waited for Mama to finish cleaning, Eunice played with David, Mrs. Miller's son. Sometimes, when Mrs. Miller drove Mama home at the end of the day, David came over so he and Eunice could spend more time together.

One day, David didn't come to play.

And the next time Eunice visited, Mrs. Miller led her son away. She had decided that it wouldn't do for David to play with a little Black girl.

There was nothing to be done.

To help pay for Eunice's piano lessons, Miss Mazzy and Mrs. Miller spread the word about her talent. They collected money in church and wrote about Eunice in the local paper. Soon, people came to recognize Eunice on the street.

When Black folks saw her, they smiled with pride. It made her feel warm and good.

When white folks saw Eunice, they pointed and said, "That's Miss Mazzy's colored girl!" which did not feel good at all.

The only other times white folks seemed to notice her was when they didn't want her around.

It was another thing Eunice didn't understand.
Another hurt she pushed down deep.

One spring Sunday, as a thank-you to all of the people who supported her, Eunice gave a concert at the Tryon Library. Daddy and Mama sat up front so they could watch her hands as she played.

Eunice was ready to begin, when a man made her parents stand so a white couple could sit. Then the man led her parents away.

Eunice waited. *Are Daddy and Mama coming back?*

The audience grew restless.

Eunice was still.

A wave of anger rolled toward her, but she hardly felt it.

At last, the white couple stood, and Daddy and Mama returned to their front-row seats. Some white people laughed as their anger cooled. But as Eunice looked at her parents' bowed heads, her anger was just getting warm.

After high school, Eunice left Miss Mazzy and North
Carolina for the Juilliard School of Music and New York City.
She lived on 145th Street in Harlem. It was fast and loud and
full of good-smelling food. The people were so elegant and
fine, Eunice wore her best dress every day just to keep up.

Eunice had a plan. If she worked hard at Juilliard, in a year she would be good enough for the real prize: the famous Curtis Institute of Music in Philadelphia. Eunice was so sure of her plan that her whole family moved to Philly before she even auditioned.

On the day of her audition, Eunice played each piece of music
from memory. She was flawless.

But it wasn't enough. The Curtis Institute turned her away.

Days later, Eunice heard from her brother,

who heard from their uncle,

who heard from his Philadelphia friends

that the Curtis Institute had rejected Eunice because she was Black.

Eunice didn't know if the rumor was true, but it *felt* true. That old familiar anger and hurt came rushing back. And for the first time, Eunice wondered whether being Black meant an end to all of her dreams.

Eunice gave up music. She worked in a photography studio and didn't play a single note. But the music inside her couldn't be ignored.

She became a piano teacher, and her students told her about New Jersey bars that hired piano players in the summer. She decided to see for herself and found her way to a rough Atlantic City club. The piano was shoved in a corner, under an umbrella to protect it from a leak. Eunice took the job.

The first night, Eunice wore a delicate dress and walked in like a queen. She opened with a Bach concerto, but this was not a Bach-friendly crowd. So Eunice played the popular songs of the day, sneaking in some Bach where she could. When she got more confident, she mixed in some of Daddy's good-time jazz, and now and then took the bar to church.

And then she sang. In a voice that was rich, sweet, and like soft thunder.

Eunice played until the sun rose. When she was thirsty, she ordered some milk. If the crowd was too loud, Eunice stopped playing, sipped her milk, and waited for quiet. She could wait all night if she had to. The milk was free.

Each night there were more people in the bar than the night before. They couldn't get enough! But this was unholy music in an unholy place, and Eunice knew Mama wouldn't approve. To keep her secret safe, she changed her name to Nina Simone.

The next year, Nina played clubs all over Atlantic City and Philadelphia. She added a new song: a Billie Holiday hit about a man named Porgy and a woman named Bess. Billie sang it sad and blue, but Nina made it dark and deep. She put it on a record, and people loved it!

Ms. Simone had arrived!

But while Nina sang of love, something else stirred in the streets of Philadelphia. A low rumble of anger and fear—the sound of Black people rising, rising, unwilling to accept being treated as less than human. It was part of a larger chorus that could be heard in New York, Chicago, and all throughout the South.

Nina heard it. Underneath the applause and growing praise, Nina heard the steady roar of unrest. Her friends—great writers and thinkers—wanted her to add her voice. She was famous now, and people would listen!

But fame was still new to Nina. She worked so hard to keep that spotlight lit, and she was exhausted. How could she join a movement when she could hardly move?

In 1963, Nina's hard work paid off. She was the main attraction at Carnegie Hall, that spectacular New York theater every musician hoped to play. Miss Mazzy came to see Nina's name in lights. Daddy came, too. Even Mama was there, sitting close enough to see Nina's hands.

Nina played eighteen songs. At the sound of the last note, the audience was on its feet, clapping, cheering, shouting for more. It was the stuff of dreams.

Except . . .

Hundreds of miles away, Dr. Martin Luther King Jr. sat in a Birmingham jail. He had marched the streets of that Alabama city, demanding respect and dignity. Instead, he and his followers were hosed, beaten, and arrested.

And that steady, rising roar grew—louder, faster, until at last it became the anguished beat of a single drum.

It sounded on June 12, 1963, when Medgar Evers, who demanded justice for Black people, was killed in Jackson, Mississippi, by a white man. When Medgar's killer stood trial, the governor of Mississippi shook his hand.

The drum sounded again on September 15, when a Black church was bombed in Birmingham and Addie Mae Collins, Cynthia Wesley, Carole Robertson, and Carol Denise McNair were killed. Nina's own little girl had just turned one year old.

The drumbeat was relentless, demanding. Its steady rhythm tugged at the hurt Nina had tucked away for so long, and set it free.

Nina pushed all of it into a raging storm of song. She called out Alabama and Mississippi by name. Her lyrics were so fed up and true, they couldn't be spoken in polite company.

But Nina was done being polite. As far as she could tell, politeness had gotten her people nothing.

Nina's voice broke with the weight of this new music. It was harder now, rough, defiant.

Black people loved her for it. They had always loved her. But now, as they sat at lunch counters, demanding to be served; rode buses, demanding to be seated; and marched, demanding good jobs for good pay—they knew how much she truly loved them.

The white backlash, however, was swift and fierce.
People smashed her records and threatened her life.
So Nina sang louder, her voice as steady as the beat
of that relentless drum.

And when that drumbeat sounded on April 4, 1968, in Memphis, Tennessee, Black people looked to Nina to ease their pain.

"What will happen," she sang, "now that the King of Love is dead?"

Nina Simone sang the whole story of Black America
for everyone to hear. Her voice resounded with the
love, joy, and power of it all.

And when she sang of Black children—you lovely,
precious dreams—her voice sounded like hope.

About
Nina Simone

Eunice Kathleen Waymon was born in 1933 in the small town of Tryon, North Carolina. Her father, John Divine, was a musician and performer before he met Eunice's mother, Mary Kate. At the time she was born, Eunice had five siblings, and two more came after her.

All of the Waymon children learned to play the piano, but none took to it like she did. Her father taught her to play jazz, but her mother, a minister, thought the only music worth knowing was church music.

When Eunice was still in diapers, she was lying on a newspaper with musical notes written on it. According to her mother, Eunice sang the notes as if she could read them. Eunice's mother was convinced that Eunice had music on the inside.

Recognizing that with the proper training Eunice could become a preeminent concert pianist, her mother—with the help of her employer, Mrs. Miller, and Mrs. Mazzanovich, a piano teacher—carefully planned Eunice's musical education. Eunice studied with Mrs. Mazzanovich and fell in love with the music of Johann Sebastian Bach. "Bach made me dedicate my life to music," she later wrote. She thought his music was perfect.

Eunice attended Juilliard in New York City, then applied to the Curtis Institute in Philadelphia, where she hoped to continue her classical training. When she wasn't accepted, Eunice believed it was because she was Black and a woman. Though officials at Curtis have since suggested that her audition was not quite as flawless as she imagined, the Curtis Institute gave Nina an honorary degree the year before she died.

Eunice stayed in Philadelphia, took private piano lessons, and taught a few students of her own. She also supported herself by playing in bars and nightclubs in nearby Atlantic City, New Jersey. Eunice's mother had moved to Philadelphia to be closer to her, and knowing her mother wouldn't approve of her new music, Eunice adopted a stage name—Nina Simone—to keep her performances a secret. It wasn't long before she told her mother the truth. She wasn't happy about Nina's new work, but it brought in much-needed money.

Nina hadn't thought of herself as a singer, but when a bar owner told her to sing or be fired, Nina found her voice. She also found a unique style. She wove classical music and the music of the church into the popular hits of the day, then overlaid her raw and sometimes mournful voice. She was such a hit, she moved back to New York, where she played small clubs and concert halls and made records that became big hits.

While Nina was becoming a star, Black people were pushing against the laws and rules that held them back. In the South, these laws were referred to as Jim Crow. Jim Crow laws meant Black people had fewer opportunities because of the color of their skin. These laws didn't have the same name in the North, but they existed there, too. In fact, in 1966 when Dr. King marched for fair housing in Chicago, he said, "I've been in many demonstrations all across the South, but I can say that I have never seen, even in Mississippi and Alabama, mobs as hostile and as hate-filled as I'm seeing in Chicago." Black people risked their lives to change these laws, and many were killed for their efforts. This fight for change is known as the Civil Rights Movement.

As Nina's fame grew, she became friends with prominent Black writers, artists, and musicians. Many of them, like novelist James Baldwin, poet Langston Hughes, and playwright Lorraine Hansberry, were civil rights activists. They encouraged Nina to join the cause, but Nina was focused on her career. Her fans expected her to play love songs, not songs of protest. But when Medgar Evers, a civil rights leader in Mississippi, was killed and the 16th Street Baptist Church was bombed in Alabama, killing four young girls, Nina could no longer be silent about what was happening to Black people in America.

For the rest of her life, Nina fought for freedom through her music. She protested the conditions Black people lived under, and demanded change through song. She also celebrated being Black. Her song, "Young, Gifted and Black," inspired by Lorraine Hansberry, became a civil rights anthem.

In the end, the laws in the United States changed, the protests quieted for a while, and people weren't as interested in protest music. But Nina knew the change wasn't real and lasting. She left the United States, finally settling in France, where she died in 2003.

Nina's music has never gone away. In 2020, when George Floyd, Breonna Taylor, Ahmaud Arbery, and others were murdered, people took to the streets around the world in protest. And many turned to Nina's music for comfort and strength.

My father, a civil rights leader in his own right, introduced me to the music of Nina Simone. He first heard her music playing in a gas station in Alabama. The song was "I Loves You, Porgy," from George and Ira Gershwin's musical *Porgy and Bess*. When my father asked the gas station attendant who was singing, the attendant replied, "I don't know if it's *Nine-ah Simon* or *Nina Simone*, but she sure can sing."

I've heard that story so often, it feels like part of who I am. So does the music of Nina Simone.

BIBLIOGRAPHY

BOOKS

Cohodas, Nadine. *Princess Noire: The Tumultuous Reign of Nina Simone.* Chapel Hill, NC: University of North Carolina Press, 2012.

Light, Alan. *What Happened, Miss Simone?* New York: Penguin Random House LLC, 2016.

Simone, Nina, and Stephen Cleary. *I Put a Spell on You: The Autobiography of Nina Simone.* New York: Da Capo Press, 1991.

MOVIES

Nina Simone: La Légende. Directed by Frank Lords. 1992. UK: BBC, 1992. TV movie.

What Happened, Miss Simone? Directed by Liz Garbus. 2015. USA: Netflix. DVD.

VIDEO

Simone, Nina. "Nina Simone: Take Me to the Water." Filmed June 1969. YouTube video, 7:34. Posted February 2013. https://www.youtube.com/watch?v=N1xWFo8xEu8.